Moods

*What Christians Should Know About
Depression, Anxiety*

Table of Contents

Introduction 3

1. Isn't there more to our moods than brain chemistry?. 6

2. Has depression become an epidemic? 11

3. What is depression? 16

4. What causes depression? 19

5. What are the symptoms of depression? 24

6. How does depression affect marriages? 31

7. Does menopause or P.M.S.
   cause depression? 32

8. Is adolescent depression just
   a normal phase? 34

9. Is it normal for the elderly to be
   depressed? 36

10. What is manic depression? 37

11. How does depression affect Christians?...................40

12. Why are Christians so difficult to treat?.....................43

13. How can depression be treated? 47

14. What is A.D.D. or hyperactivity?............................... 55

15. What happens if you don't treat A.D.D? 61

16. What is schizophrenia? 64

17. What is anxiety disorder and obsessive
    compulsive disorder?...67

18. What can be done for anorexia nervosa,
    chronic fatigue and fibromyalgia? 70

19. Conclusion 72

20. Symptom Checklist 74

INTRODUCTION

This book has been written to help Christians better understand the most common medical conditions that affect thinking and feeling. Christians are often very confused about the nature and treatment of mental illness. People are also very suspicious of psychiatric treatments, so many are suffering needlessly from correctable conditions.

This book will explain all the psychiatry that you need to know to remove the mystery, misunderstanding, confusion and stigma attached to the mood disorders, namely, depression, anxiety and bipolar disorder. Attention Deficit and other common mental health conditions will be discussed.

As you will learn in the next chapter, there are three parts to humans: body, soul and spirit. Each aspect contributes to our emotions. To become emotionally well, each part needs to be examined and treated if necessary.

This book deals only with physical conditions that affect our thinking and feeling. It explains the medical conditions, their treatments and why Christians no longer need to be afraid of modern psychiatric medications.

For a more complete discussion of the healing processes for body, soul and spirit, read *Emotionally Free,* published in North America by Chosen Books and internationally by Sovereign World (ISBN 1 85240 365 9). You can see it in the Resource Centre of our web site at www.drgrantmullen.com.

The following pages will answer the most common questions that I've been asked in my mental health clinic. After completing the book you will be able to recognize and understand these conditions and know how to get help. You will then have the tools to help yourself or a suffering loved one return to normal functioning. You will also be better able to support someone going through the treatment process by giving them a reason to be hopeful.

Medical research in recent years has provided physicians with very effective tools to treat these common conditions. These treatments however are not reaching the people who need them because of lack of awareness or understanding in the general public.

The current situation is similar to the era when eye glasses were first introduced. They were a very effective treatment for blurred vision but they were not well received by the public since people had no idea that they themselves had blurred vision and could be helped with glasses. Most had learned to live with their poor vision and ridiculed those who did wear glasses. I'm sure that there were those who said "if God wanted me to see better he would have made me that way, there's no need to wear those ugly things on my face." In those days one could function quite well with poor vision since transportation was with horses and the animals always knew the way home even if the driver didn't.

Those who tried the glasses couldn't believe the improvement and wished that they had started wearing them years before. Their

"In those days people thought they could function well with poor vision."

vision became normal but they had to live with the stigma attached to wearing glasses. The people around them didn't realize how much better the person's vision had become since blurred vision was an invisible handicap. It was easy and popular to criticize the ugly glasses.

Now we are dealing with problems of "blurred" thinking, which are invisible to an observer. Even the sufferer doesn't know that he is not thinking as clearly as he should be. The victim is so accustomed to this disability that he doesn't know he has a problem. He is then resistant to the suggestion that he could be helped and even ridicules those who do go for help. This book will allow anyone to "measure" his thinking pattern and determine if there is any "blurring" which could be corrected.

This information, of course, does not replace a proper evaluation by a physician or counsellor but it will assist in the evaluation process.

Chapter 1
Isn't there more to our moods than brain chemistry?

As I mentioned in the introduction, there are three parts to humans and three parts to our recovery. Medication for chemical imbalance mood disorders is only one of the three recovery paths.

Throughout the course of everyone's life, emotional chains or wounds are accumulated as the result of negative events and stresses. These emotional injuries cause personality damage which keeps people trapped in the bondage of negative, destructive thought patterns. The dysfunctional thought patterns interfere with daily activities and damage relationships. The accumulated wounds and

Everyone has baggage.

memories fill our emotional "baggage" that we carry with us until emotional recovery takes place. The thought-cluttering from mood disorders greatly magnifies the bondage caused by these emotional chains.

At the time of conversion, God accepts everyone as they are—chained, broken and wounded. The Holy Spirit is available to help Christians break these chains of the past and heal the wounded personality. This process however, is voluntary. It will only happen if the believer permits it. This is the process of sanctification or refining, which is God's intention for every believer.

You will learn in this book how medications can effectively restore thought control and concentration when a mood disorder is present. They do not however, break emotional chains, negative behavioral patterns or occult attacks.

For complete emotional inner healing, God's power is required to break the chains and heal the wounded personality. It is very difficult though, to apply God's truth to your inner self until concentration is restored through the use of medications or divine healing. After this is completed, it is God's intention for the Holy Spirit to complete the task of setting each believer free of their chains. This is accomplished by applying the truth of God's word with the power of the Spirit.

I have already mentioned that there are three parts to humans, body, soul and spirit. Each of these parts can be bound in dysfunction that will affect our moods. I like to think that when bound, each of the three parts can be represented by a link in a chain of emotional bondage. In the following diagram you will see that there are three links in the chain of emotional bondage which correspond to the three parts of humans. Each link must be addressed if full restoration of the mind and soul is to take place. If any of the three areas are ignored, then recovery will be incomplete. Each area has an effect on the other two areas since they are all interdependent.

The "Chemical" link refers to physical causes that result in abnormalities of mood and thought control. These imbalances must be corrected medically before significant progress can be made in the other two areas. This book specifically addresses problems with chemical imbalances.

The "Woundedness" link refers to all of the personality damage that has been accumulated during a person's lifetime. These wounds create thought patterns that shape our personality, habits, attitudes and behaviors. Many of these thought patterns are based on lies that have infiltrated our minds without our knowledge. Incorrect attitudes are then formed which influence our behavior and relationships. Inner Healing refers to the process of breaking the emotional chains and healing the wounds that have accumulated from our past. It addresses attitudes, behaviors and relationships.

There are many authors who explain how to recognize woundedness and how the Holy Spirit can set one free. The best results are usually obtained when you are reading the books recommended by your therapist. Inner healing proceeds much faster when

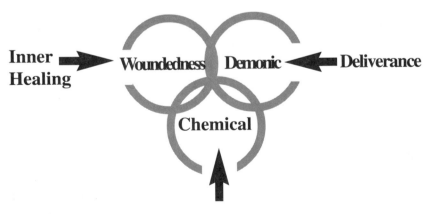

Medications/Divine Healing

The Chains of Emotional Bondage

you are working with a Christian counsellor who will guide you in addressing all three links in the chain of emotional bondage.

What about Spiritual Attack?

The "Demonic" link refers to bondage that has resulted from the spiritual attack of evil spirits. This may result from past or present personal sin, being the victim of sin or inherited generational curses. There are many other sources of this kind of bondage. Deliverance is the process of breaking free of the influence of evil spirits that want to influence thoughts and behavior. There are many books and ministries that can help in this area.

Spiritual attack is a very real issue, especially in depressed Christians. The loss of concentration and the cluttering of negative thoughts make a person particularly vulnerable to occult influences.

When a person's mind is filled with negative discouraging thoughts that can't be shut off, then it is very easy for Satan to insert even more condemning thoughts or suggestions in among the person's own thoughts. The depressed person is unable to detect the intrusion of lies, condemnation or misinterpretations from an evil source and just assumes that the thoughts are his own. The inserted thoughts are intended to magnify the pain of depression and to separate the victim from supportive friends, counsellors and most of all, from God. When concentration is impaired by depression, it is very difficult to "take every thought captive" and block the intrusion of dark thoughts.

This state is much like having a house with no doors or windows covering the holes in the walls. The house is always filling with dirt or debris that is blowing by. It is impossible to keep the house clean. When a mind is racing and cluttered, there is very little defence against evil, disturbing thoughts that are directed against that person. These thoughts will just "blow in" and fill part of the house. A poorly protected mind will accumulate many unwanted negative thoughts, especially the kind that separate a person from God.

When a person recovers from depression, it is much like putting glass and doors over all the holes to keep out unwanted thoughts. In this way, thought control is restored and any thoughts of an evil origin are quickly detected and disposed of. The mind can then be kept clean since the entry points are controlled and monitored.

In my experience, the first step in the process of deliverance or becoming free from the harassment of evil, is to treat any depression that may be present. When thought control and concentration is restored, then believers can use their authority over Satan and he will flee. I strongly recommend the books by Neil Anderson like *The Bondage Breaker,* to help a person learn how to use their authority in deliverance once their mood has been restored.

There is a great deal more information about emotional bondage, spiritual authority and how to use it to protect your thoughts in the book *Emotionally Free.*

Chapter 2
Has depression become an epidemic?

How common is depression?

Of all the different kinds of chemical imbalance mood disorders that we will discuss, depression is by far the most common.

Depression is one of the most undiagnosed and disabling medical conditions in society today. According to many studies, it costs the U.S. economy approximately $27 billion annually in medical costs, lost productivity, unemployment, increased susceptibility to illness, suicide, family disruption, relationship failure, alcohol abuse and personal suffering. The Canadian costs are estimated at $5 billion annually.

Mental disorders cause a much broader degree of disability than most other medical conditions like back pain, diabetes and heart disease. A psychiatric condition affects all levels of functioning as compared to other diseases that only affect one organ system. Insurance companies are now very concerned at the staggering number of disability claims that are being submitted due to emotional disability. There are several corporations in Canada who realize that mental disability has become for them the most common cause of days off work due to illness. They have started prevention and early detection programs for their employees.

Depression is more disabling than most chronic illnesses. Even though there are now very effective treatments available, most people with depression remain undiagnosed and untreated due to lack of awareness and not accepting depression as a legitimate illness.

The unnecessary suffering often continues for a lifetime, causing intense mental, emotional and physical anguish, disrupting all relationships both at home and work.

If a person acknowledges this condition and goes for help, they then must endure the unfair stigma of an uninformed public that presumes that depression is a character defect, lack of will power or a personal weakness. Not only does a depressed person have to cope with the illness but also with the scorn of society. No other chronic illness is treated so unfairly by the public.

Six to ten percent of the population is depressed at any given time. This very common condition is undiagnosed and untreated in eighty percent of its victims.

Depressed people have to endure misunderstanding.

The problem with the Y chromosome

Depression is more common in women due to poorly understood genetic factors. It is not because they are the "weaker sex" or because emotional issues are "women's problems." There are some medical conditions that are more common to one sex or the other. Heart disease for example is more common in males for genetic reasons only. It has been estimated that ten to twenty percent of women will at some time in their lives have symptoms of chemical imbalance depression. The condition for the majority of them will usually be mild and remain untreated but that means that there are a very large number of untreated women who are not feeling as well as they could be.

The lifetime risk for men is a much more difficult statistic to estimate. When I first started treating depression, the lifetime risk for depression in men was four percent. The number has now climbed closer to ten percent in the past fifteen years. I'm not convinced that men are more depressed now than they were when I started practicing. I think the difference has come due to improved detection techniques for the symptoms of depression in men. It is much more difficult to diagnose depression in men and I have a theory as to why that is so.

We know that the difference between the sexes in the incidence of depression is due to genetic factors The genetic difference between males and females is that males have a Y chromosome that females don't have. After many years of observation of men and through being one myself, I have come to the conclusion that the Y chromosome is likely made of "denial!" It is extremely difficult to get a man to admit he is depressed or to accept treatment.

In my years of practice I have noticed a profound difference in how men and women suffer with depression. When a woman is depressed, she will usually come to my office and complain that there is something wrong, that it is her fault and she wants help to fix the problem. When a man is depressed, if he comes to the office at all, which in itself is rare, he will say that there is something wrong, it's the fault of his wife and would I please fix her.

Instead of admitting to the problem, he will run from it, busy himself, watch TV or abuse alcohol to distract himself from the discomfort. It is very frustrating to try and get men into treatment for depression.

Depression is more common as people age and unfortunately the elderly assume that it is normal to be depressed and don't come for treatment. It is found in all races and social classes, even occur-

The Y chromosome is made of denial.

ring in those who are not stressed and are otherwise completely well.

All disorders of mood are strongly inherited. If one parent has depression, there is a thirty percent risk that a child will also become depressed. If both parents are depressed the risk may rise to seventy five percent.

Depression is not a benign illness. Fifteen percent of untreated, severely depressed people will commit suicide and eighty percent of all those who commit suicide have a treatable mental illness. This means that there are a very large number of preventable

14

suicide deaths.

At least ten percent (some researchers say twenty percent) of the population will suffer from a mood disorder at some time in their life. Most will not be treated because of the stigma attached to the diagnosis and treatment. Stigma is the single most important obstacle to treatment. Sufferers are afraid to report their symptoms due to the negative consequences that may come in their work and family as a result of their diagnosis.

Effective treatment will only begin when a person recognizes the problem and overcomes the obstacles to treatment. Through public education, awareness of these conditions should increase and the stigma attached to these illnesses should dissolve.

Depressed people are shunned.

Chapter 3
What is depression?

Isn't depression a normal part of life?

Sue was seventeen and in high school. She was struggling like everyone else her age to fit in and be accepted. This particular year she was not getting along with her friends and she had not been invited to any of their parties. Sue was feeling hurt and left out. School was the only activity in her life that she enjoyed and her grades were excellent. Sue felt depressed.

Bob was thirty, a successful accountant until the last few years. He was finding it harder to do his usual work. He couldn't keep his mind on anything long enough to complete it. He was always tired. Bob was getting increasingly worried about insignificant things. Every pain he experienced made him wonder about cancer. He would lie awake at night, unable to stop worrying if he had made any errors in his work the previous day. Life was becoming a struggle and he was losing his will to continue the battle each day to survive. He just didn't seem interested in his work or family anymore. Bob felt depressed.

Both Bob and Sue felt depressed but there was a vast difference between their situations. The general public does not correctly differentiate between normal and abnormal "depression." If we are going to help those who need it most, we must be able to tell who is suffering from the illness of depression.

Depression is by far the most common form of mental suffering. It is however, a poorly defined condition which means different things to different people. We must be able to distinguish between the transient "depression" of someone unhappy about a recent disappointment (Sue) and the severe crushing despair of one who has for many years lost all interest in life (Bob). I choose to use the term "discouragement" for temporary mood fluctuations which would be commonly referred to as the "blues" and would never be considered an "illness." "Depression" is reserved for prolonged disorders of mood that require professional help.

It is not always easy to distinguish between these two conditions and it requires considerable training and experience. There is presently no blood test or X-ray that will diagnose mental illness. Understanding what a person is thinking and feeling is the only way to separate these conditions. This difficulty in making the diagnosis has caused enormous difficulty in getting the right people into treatment.

At this time we have no screening tool to use on the population to find all those who are depressed needing help. It is much easier to find people with vision impairment since the vision screening chart is widely available and well accepted by the public. Our ability to

Someday we might have a test for depression.

diagnose depression depends on a person's ability to describe what they are thinking to someone who understands illnesses of mood. This requires a significant level of insight, motivation and verbal skill. There are many sufferers who are just unable to communicate their thoughts and so they remain untreated. Since we have no test, we cannot prove that someone has a depressive illness. This allows skeptics to influence a depressed person not to accept treatment or to accept another explanation of their symptoms. The inability to measure mood causes the public to see psychiatric treatment as unreliable, unpredictable, "hocus pocus" and to be avoided. It is a constant struggle for physicians to try to convince sufferers that there is a scientific and reliable treatment for something that cannot be measured scientifically. Therefore, I will try to describe the differences between true depression and what I call discouragement.

Discouragement is transient, with an obvious cause, and the person is still able to enjoy other unrelated activities. It resolves with time and supportive counselling. A discouraged person can still be hopeful, with good thought control and concentration. In our example, Sue had recently felt badly about her circumstances but she still did well at school which required great concentration. She met the criteria for normal discouragement over life events.

Depression is usually very prolonged with unrelenting symptoms. It is often, though not always characterized by sadness. There is an inability to enjoy activities and all interests fade. There is general hopelessness and a lack of ability to control or steer thoughts. This is a much more disabling condition than discouragement. Bob was truly depressed. He had been suffering for years; his concentration and thought control were worsening. He was losing interest in all of life. Bob needed medical treatment and counselling. Sue likely only needed a friend, or at the most, counselling.

Chapter 4
What causes depression?

Can't they just "snap out of it"?

The brain is divided into regions or "control centres" that direct every activity of the body. I have attempted to illustrate these regions in Figure 1. These control centres work independently of conscious thought to regulate your body automatically. For example, your pupil size is adjusted continuously by one of these control centres, yet you have no control over it whatsoever.

In the movement control centre, nerve cells communicate with each other and with muscle cells to create movement. This process is initiated by a thought of intention to move a limb. The nerve cells in the intention region of the brain send a command to the nerve cells which connect to the muscles to carry out the movement. If there is

Brain Control Regions

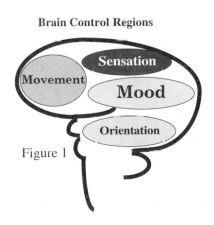

Figure 1

any kind of nerve damage or chemical imbalance in the movement control nerves, there will be no transmitted signal, nor will there be movement. Nothing will move even though there may be a very strong intentional thought to move the limb. This is the situation after a stroke. The intention to move is there but nothing moves due a nerve injury.

You only have voluntary control of your limbs if all your nerve cells are working correctly to give you that control in response to a thought of intention. If any nerves in the chain of command are not functioning correctly, nothing moves, regardless of the intensity of the intention.

This situation can be illustrated if you consider a high performance sports car fueled and ready to go. The highly skilled driver takes his seat, pulls out his maps and waves to the crowd who is encouraging him on. The conditions for driving are perfect. When the driver attempts to pull out of the driveway he discovers that the steering wheel is not connected to the wheels. How far is he going now?

In this scenario, there are very strong intentions but nothing happens since there is an internal invisible problem that takes con-

How far can you go without a steering wheel?

trol of the vehicle away from the driver.

It is important to realize that forming a thought is as physical an event as blinking an eye or moving your arm. Nerve cells in the brain allow you to form thoughts in the same way that they permit movement. We only have full control of our thoughts when all the nerve cells are working properly to give us that control. This process is subject to malfunction like any other part of the body. We can lose voluntary control of our thoughts if we have an internal neurological malfunction or an imbalance of nerve transmitter chemicals even though we may have the best of intentions to control our thoughts.

The mood control centre which is illustrated below, is the place in the brain where thought content and thought speed are regulated. This centre controls what you think about and how fast you think about it. It therefore controls mood and concentration. We don't know where it is located in the brain since it is more of a function than a location.

If your nerve cells are working correctly in this location, your

Mood Control Centre

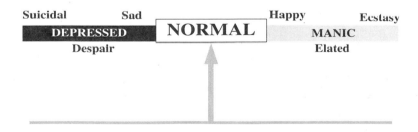

The Mood Control Centre should maintain mood in the normal range regardless of circumstances.

mood and concentration will always be kept within the normal range. It is impossible to measure mood but we define normal mood as being relaxed, content, feeling in control, concentrating normally, clear headed and coping with stress. I'm not sure that I know anyone this normal; they would likely stick out from the population and be very dull. When the control centre is functioning well, your mood will always eventually return to the normal range regardless of the degree of negative stress which would be depressing, or positive stress which would be exhilarating. It works much like a top or gyroscope that will always return to the vertical position as long as it is spinning.

There are very specific chemical substances called neurotransmitters that are produced by brain cells to regulate these control functions. If anything happens to disrupt the production of these chemicals, then the control centre will malfunction and mood will fluctuate outside of the normal range and you will lose the ability to control your thoughts. If for example, there is a chemical imbalance, you would find your thoughts going faster and it would be harder to control what you were thinking about. If something positive happened, your thoughts could race uncontrollably in excitement or if something bad happened, you could race with depressive thoughts. You would lose the ability to put brakes on the thoughts.

It is now well established that mental illnesses are usually the result of an imbalance in the chemicals associated with mood control. This tendency to malfunction is usually inherited. Symptoms may just appear without reason or depression may come as a result of stressful circumstances that bring out the inherited tendency to have a mood disorder. As a result of the discovery of the above facts, depression is now seen as a physical illness needing and responding to medical treatment.

Due to the genetic nature of the condition, a triggering stress is not always needed. Sometimes depression just develops over years with no obvious cause. There is no doubt however, that stress can trigger a depressive illness in someone who already has the genetic potential for depression. If there is very strong genetic potential, then it will take very little stress to trigger an illness and symptoms may appear at an early age. If the genetic link is weaker, then more stress is needed to cause disability and the condition may not appear until late in life, if at all.

The treatment of depression is the same whether or not it was triggered by stress. If the chemical imbalance is present, it can be treated regardless of the cause. Think of it this way. If someone breaks their leg, they will need a cast. It doesn't matter if it was caused by a fall or a car accident, the treatment of the resulting disability is the same.

When the chemical imbalance is corrected, the person is then better able to deal with their stresses since their thought control has been restored.

Chapter 5
What are the symptoms of depression?

How does a depressed person feel?

Depression has a very wide variety of symptoms and each individual shows a different pattern. Generally speaking, these people usually have been sad for prolonged periods without obvious cause. The onset of depressive symptoms is usually very slow and insidious so a person doesn't realize that they are slowly sliding into depression. They just gradually adjust to an ever worsening mood and assume that they are reacting normally to life's circumstances. The onset of depression is often during the teen years, but at that time the symptoms may be dismissed as just an "adolescent phase" (see chapter 8).

In my clinic, after someone has recovered from depression, I always ask them when was the last time they felt as well as they did after treatment. The answer is commonly, "I have never felt this well in my life" or "not for at least twenty years." This was a shock to me in my early years, but it illustrated how gradually the condition takes hold, and how people just get used to being depressed.

Depressed people lose interest in most activities of life that previously gave them pleasure. They feel defeated, useless, hopeless, unable to pray, punished by God, and unworthy of anyone's love or God's forgiveness. They may feel that God has left them, or is no longer listening to them due to unknowingly committing the "unpardonable sin." They consider themselves to be a failure as a Christian and as a person. Plagued by guilt, they condemn themselves for not being able to "snap out of it." Some have increased irritability and will attack everyone around them as the likely cause for their unhappiness. They find it hard to relax or ever feel content. There is a diminished interest in sex or any kind of intimacy.

Depressed people often have great difficulty falling asleep due to persistent and uncontrollable racing of unpleasant thoughts or worries through their mind. Many will awaken at four a.m. and will be unable to fall asleep again because of the same racing of thoughts. Others oversleep and use it as an escape from an unpleasant reality Concentration on work, pleasure or reading becomes impossible while struggling with the continuous stream of unpleasant and depressing thoughts that cannot be kept out of the mind. When reading, they will see the words, but have to reread the sentence many times before understanding what was said. It is hard for them to keep their minds on anything. Their memory seems to fail and it becomes very difficult to finish any project due to fatigue or lack of interest.

Fatigue becomes overwhelming in eighty percent of depressed people. Daily responsibilities which were previously easy and pleasant are seen as enormous undertakings. Everything becomes such an effort that activities are avoided. A depressed person also finds it very hard to make decisions since their self confidence is so low and concentration is so impaired. Anxiety becomes a continuous thought

Suicidal	Sad		Happy	Ecstasy
DEPRESSED		NORMAL	MANIC	
Despair			Elated	

Chemical imbalance prevents the Mood Control Centre from restoring normal mood.

pattern which cannot be turned off. The depressed person will worry about everything, even tiny details of life that never before attracted their attention. Fifty percent of depressed people can't stop worrying. Intense fear and worry may induce unusual behavior patterns, like repetitive hand washing, to rid themselves of a sensation of being dirty. This is also known as Obsessive Compulsive Disorder (O.C.D.) (see chapter 17).

There may be a preoccupation with body symptoms and frequent visits to doctors with complaints that can never be diagnosed or treated. Chronic pain is often present and it hides the underlying depression. Medical treatment is then directed at the pain, so the mood remains untreated and the emotional disability continues undetected. Sixty percent of chronic pain patients have a medical depression, but they may hide behind the legitimacy of pain to prevent the detection of a less socially acceptable condition.

Socialization is difficult during depression and it becomes very uncomfortable to attend church. Depressed people find that they don't get anything out of church services and often complain that

Depressive thought patterns can take many forms.

they "aren't being fed." They have multiple complaints about the pastor or members. It is very common for them to change churches frequently in search of a congregation that will fill their needs.

Crying becomes a frequent event. There is a tendency to blame others, especially spouse, family members or God for their state of unhappiness.

All of the above symptoms by themselves are common and do not always indicate a mental illness. When however, a number of these signs are present continuously for over two months, then treatable illness must be suspected.

The onset of depression is often during the teen years, but at that time the symptoms are dismissed as just an "adolescent phase" (see chapter 8). Most of my patients have been suffering for over ten years before they realize that help is available. The onset is so insidious that it goes unnoticed and the person and their family just adjust to the changes. It becomes the new normal for that person, so they sense no need of corrective treatment.

Depression affects every part of our ability to think and feel. It clouds our personality and changes how we interpret events, and how

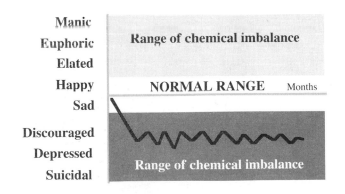

The onset of depression is insidious and can continue undetected for a lifetime.

we relate to others. It magnifies physical pain, disrupts relationships, blocks communication and changes our eating and sleeping patterns. It also affects everyone around us in a negative way. There are very few illnesses known that cut such a broad path of devastation and disability. It is a very common condition, but it often goes undiagnosed since there is no confirmatory test, and it can be masked by chronic pain, fatigue and burnout.

One common type of depression only occurs during the winter months. It is called "Seasonal Affective Disorder" or "S.A.D." In this depression, a person can be totally symptom free in the summer, but will notice a drop in mood every fall. During the winter months the symptoms are identical to conventional depression but they remit spontaneously in the spring. These sufferers may only need medications during the winter months. Light therapy is also effective in some people. It involves sitting in front of a special type of lamp for several hours daily in place of taking medications.

It has been my observation that most of those who have come to my clinic suspecting that they had S.A.D., did in fact have depression symptoms year round, but were only aware of them in the winters. They responded best to continuous year round treatment rather

Depression is an invisible handicap.

than winter only medications.

Dysthymia

Most cases of depression are mild. When symptoms are mild, most people ignore them and are never treated so it leaves them chronically emotionally disabled but unaware of it. Researchers estimate that at least six percent of the population are chronically unhappy, in a state of mild depression. This state of mild depression has now been termed "Dysthymia." People with this form of depression are very susceptible to becoming severely depressed with advancing years or increasing stress. Dysthymics often suffer from chronic vague physical symptoms that don't easily fit medical symptom models like persisting headache, abdominal pain, poor sleep, fatigue and poor appetite. They can't be easily diagnosed or treated since their prob lems are so ill defined. Dysthymics also have chronically poor relationships.

Once again we can draw a comparison to vision abnormalities. Most short-sighted people have only mild symptoms; very few ever need a "white cane" which indicates blindness. We commonly, however, prescribe glasses to the mildly impaired since we know it will help them with reading and driving and improve their quality of life. The same should be the case in mood disorders. Mildly depressed people should also be treated since their disability is definitely interfering with their lives and relationships. Unfortunately, this group is the hardest to detect and the most difficult to convince to get help. Mild depression and dysthymia responds to the same treatment as severe depression. A symptom checklist for dysthymia can be found in chapter 20. With any of those checklists, you will be able to diagnose yourself, or a loved one, and know if medical treatment is needed. These kinds of depression are broadly referred to as unipolar depressions.

Why do people commit suicide?

Depression is a potentially fatal illness and unfortunately, suicide is common. Up to twenty percent of depressed people will attempt suicide. Some researchers estimate that fifteen percent of untreated, depressed people will kill themselves.

When people consider or plan suicide, it's because they become overwhelmed with hopelessness and see death as the only escape from the torment of their present reality. Depressed people are much more likely to commit suicide if they are abusing drugs or alcohol, if they have another serious illness, if they have recently experienced a major loss in their lives or are under significant stress. People who have previously attempted suicide are more likely to commit suicide at a later date.

Many who attempt or talk about suicide are actually calling out for help. It is at this point that we should take the threat seriously and guide them into treatment. It is wrong and dangerous to ignore them believing that "it's only a cry for help; they won't do it." Many lives would be saved if we could intervene at this stage.

If you are concerned about the risk of suicide in someone you love, watch for any of these classical warning signs. A person's mood may rapidly decline so that they are preoccupied with hopelessness and despair. Watch for reckless behavior that is out of character, where they no longer care about consequences. Some will become more socially withdrawn, lose interest in activities or friends, stop eating and give away important possessions. The most obvious signs would be a rewritten will, insurance application or openly discussing death. If you see these signs, the person is in need of urgent medical assistance. Don't ignore them!

If someone has recently attempted suicide, they will need a great deal of love and support, since they suffer from an added burden of guilt and shame on top of the preexisting depression.

Chapter 6
How does depression affect marriages?

Dave and Mary (fictitious characters) married in their early twenties and had a wonderful relationship for many years. Over the past five years however, Dave had become increasingly sad and worried. He had lost interest in his career, in going to church and in socializing. He blamed it on becoming forty and on the financial pressures he lived under. In the past year he lost interest in his own children. He blamed God for the state of his life and he rarely talked to Mary. This year he told Mary that he was no longer in love with her and that they should consider separation. Mary was shocked, devastated and didn't know what to do.

Dave was suffering from a gradual onset of depression which was steadily worsening. He didn't recognize that he was ill, since he had learned to live with it for so long. He found many sources of stress on which to blame his deteriorating mood, so he thought his response was reasonable and logical. His depression was disrupting his work and marriage. If he didn't get help his marriage was finished.

Depression, and all mood disorders, disrupt relationships both inside and outside the home. Marriages are severely strained by the temper, irritability, fatigue and apathy found in a depressed spouse. Twenty percent of all marriages are unhappy. In fifty percent of those unhappy couples, one or both spouses have a mood disorder. In my clinic, one of the most common causes of marriage failure is a mood disorder in a spouse. It is so important to get depressed people treated so that marriages can be saved.

Chapter 7

Does menopause or premenstrual syndrome (P.M.S.) cause depression?

Premenstrual syndrome is a very common condition that occurs seven to fourteen days prior to the onset of a menstrual period, due to the hormonal change that takes place during that interval. It has both physical and psychological symptoms that usually clear when the period starts. Up to ten percent of women have P.M.S. mood changes severe enough to greatly interfere with their lives. Many women become profoundly depressed during the P.M.S. days. No one is certain why this is so, but some researchers have suspected that changing estrogen levels may affect the serotonin levels in the brain which control mood.

Menopause has always been blamed for causing depression and has been unkindly referred to as "mental pause." This is not so. It is not mandatory to become emotionally unstable at menopause.

There is no question that mood is affected by the hormonal fluctuations of menopause and of normal menstrual periods. These fluctuations won't however, actually cause a chemical depression. In my observation, menopause and P.M.S. tend to magnify the symptoms of a preexisting underlying depression. If for example, a woman has been suffering with a mild undiagnosed depression or dysthymia for many years, the hormonal change at menopause or during her P.M.S. days, may magnify her depressive symptoms to the point where she wants treatment. The menopause, or menstrual cycle, was not the actual cause of the depression but it aggravated the condition enough to expose it.

When women go to their doctors complaining of menopausal and depressive symptoms, they usually get treated for only the menopausal symptoms or cyclic bloating and the underlying depression is missed. It is important to treat both the menopausal and depression symptoms separately. They are both legitimate biochemical, treatable conditions. Both menopausal and P.M.S. depressions respond well to antidepressants.

There are other circumstances taking place in a menopausal woman's life that can aggravate her mood and that have nothing to do with her hormonal status. She likely has teenagers who may be already exhibiting symptoms of mild depression that they inherited from her. This will greatly increase her stress levels.

She may also be married to a man who is himself struggling with an undiagnosed depression, and being a man, would never go for help. He would far rather blame his emotions on his wife's menopause. A woman in menopause is always a convenient target for a depressed man in denial who is going through his own "mid life crisis."

Chapter 8

Is adolescent depression just a normal phase?

Virginia's parents just couldn't understand how their daughter had changed. She had been such a nice quiet girl up until age twelve. She had done well in primary school even though she was very shy and seemed to worry excessively. Now that she was in high school she had become angry, irritable, rebellious and was skipping classes. The slightest thing could set off her very bad temper. She spent too much time alone in her room listening to music. What had gone wrong? Her parents wondered if this was just part of being a teenager but it was disrupting their entire home life. Virginia was depressed.

Depression and other mood disorders are very common in the teen years, and it is estimated that up to twenty percent of teens have depressive symptoms. The rate of suicide in adolescents has risen two hundred percent in the past ten years, so it is now the third leading cause of death in that age group. Depression is not a normal developmental phase that will pass. Adolescent mood disorders cause serious disabilities in academic progress and personality development.

Most adult mood disorders begin in adolescence, but they are not detected due to the public perception that it is normal for teens to have emotional instability and that "it's just a phase." Frequently it will be assumed that a depressed, irritable teen merely has "normal youthful rebellion," and then will not be considered to have a treatable illness. This is tragic. Depressed teens will respond to medications as well as adults do, so they are suffering needlessly. Without treatment, they may have developmental, academic and social problems with destructive lifelong consequences.

The symptoms of adolescent depression are the same as in adults, with perhaps a greater degree of irritability, defiance, lack of interest in school and low self esteem. Depressed teens lose the ability to enjoy activities, they change their eating habits, complain of constant fatigue and become worried or withdrawn. They may also show antisocial behavior with stealing, fighting and trouble with the law. Depressed teens have few friends, since they are considered socially undesirable. Many will turn to drugs and alcohol to calm their minds from the constant stream of unpleasant negative thoughts. Addictions are very common in this condition. Families with depressed adolescents are often in constant turmoil and conflict due to the irritability of the teenager.

Adolescent depression is also strongly inherited. Fifty percent of children with depressed parents will also become depressed. In my experience, teens respond to the same medications that are used in adults and with the same rate of success. It is very hard however, to convince a teenager, or their parents, that medications are needed. As a result, the vast majority of adolescent mood disorders remain undiagnosed and untreated, causing years of unnecessary disability and in some cases death. In chapter 20 you will find a checklist of depressive symptoms common to adolescents. If you see these symptoms in a teenager, they need help quickly.

Chapter 9
Is it normal for the elderly to be depressed?

Depression is very common in the later years, but it is usually missed, and the symptoms wrongly attributed to normal aging. Society has come to expect depression to occur in the elderly, and so it is ignored. This is much like the neglect of adolescent depression, since it too has been considered normal for that age group.

The incidence of depression increases with age. It is presumed that this is caused by a decline in the level of nerve cell chemicals. This decline seems to be much worse if another unrelated chronic illness is present. Up to thirty percent of stroke victims will become chemically depressed. There is also an increasing level of stress and number of losses in later years which could precipitate depression. The rate of successful suicide reaches its peak in the elderly age group.

Depression can be easily confused with senility and can be found along with senility. It is important to treat depression as an independent condition since it will respond to treatment at any age.

The elderly should be treated for depression in the same aggressive way as those in other age groups. They will respond to medications too. It is important to be watching for depression in the elderly, since their quality of life, and that of their care taking relatives, can be greatly improved with proper treatment of such a common condition. There is also strong evidence that a depressed mood will predispose one to more physical illnesses. After a heart attack for example, the risk of another attack is much greater in those who are depressed.

Chapter 10
What is manic depression?

Depression is the most frequent form of mood disorder. The manic depressive, or what is now termed "bipolar" mood disorder, is the next most common. It is characterized by wide mood fluctuations ranging from deep depression and despair to extreme happiness, euphoria and mania.

During a depressed phase, bipolar depression is indistinguishable from unipolar depression. If a person is having their first episode of depression, it is not possible to tell which type of depression is present. About thirty percent of people having their first episode of depression are in fact bipolar, but the swinging mood pattern has not yet emerged.

During a manic phase a person will talk excessively and loudly with words pouring out in an animated continuous stream, interspersed with wit and humour. They will be unable to sit still or relax, and there is continuous agitation. They will be distractible, changing topics rapidly, never totally finishing one thought and over committing themselves to any task. Being the "life of the party," they show endless energy, developing grandiose plans based on gross overestimations of their own ability. Their thoughts are continuously racing with exciting plans or jobs to do that demand immediate attention. When opposed, they may show intense rage and irritability. They have poor judgment, especially when spending money. They need very little sleep, and consider rest and eating to be a waste of time, only for the weak. Lack of sleep can trigger a manic phase, and then continuing lack of sleep will fuel and intensify a manic episode. During this phase they may act totally out of character, and impulsively take risks of a sexual, personal, or financial nature. During a "high" they are very reluctant to seek treatment, since they feel so great and powerful. Manic episodes are often followed by periods of profound depression which are triggered by the slightest disappointment. A complete list of symptoms can be found in chapter 20.

Milder mood swings can also be found in bipolar illness. This condition is called cyclothymic mood disorder. There is still a fluctuating mood with racing thoughts, but the elevated mood symptoms are not as intense as the ones listed above. In this milder condition, the times of mood elevation can be very productive and entertaining. I have noticed that many actors and entertainers have this mood pattern, since it gives them the confidence to be in front of audiences. Unfortunately, the times of mood elevation are still followed by depressions.

The usual age of onset of bipolar depression is in late adolescence and the early twenties, the same as in other mood disorders. It is usually not recognized until symptoms have been present for, on average, ten years. In the years preceding diagnosis there is usually unpredictable mood and behavior with marked irritability. This is commonly seen during the adolescent prelude to being diagnosed, when this behavior is called "a normal phase." Those with bipolar

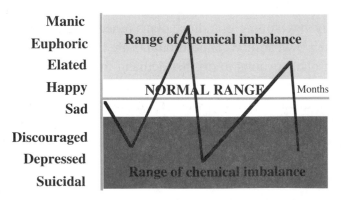

Bipolar illness causes wide mood swings.

mood disorder are very prone to abuse alcohol and street drugs as a way of self medicating their confused and tormenting thoughts.

Bipolar mood swings can easily become so severe that they slip into what is known as "psychosis." We will discuss psychosis in more detail in the chapter on schizophrenia. Psychotic thinking means that a person has lost touch with reality. It can happen at the extremes of depression or elation. A person in psychosis may hear voices when there is no one around, may feel that they are being watched or followed by strangers, or may feel that others can read their minds. They may also develop strange delusional beliefs that they have superhuman abilities. When psychotic thinking is present, it is impossible to distinguish the condition from schizophrenia. In my clinic, to separate the two conditions I ask what their mood was like in the few days leading up to the psychotic episode. If there was depression or elation, then the cause was likely a mood disorder, otherwise schizophrenia would be the probable cause.

Bipolar mood disorder responds well to treatment, as we will discuss later.

People with mania are full of energy and ideas.

Chapter 11
How does depression affect Christians?

Depression disrupts all relationships including a relationship with God. A depressed Christian will feel that they have lost the joy of their salvation and that they no longer feel God's presence. God will seem farther away, silent and unreachable. It will be very difficult to pray and do devotions since both of these acts require concentration which is disrupted by depression. The victim will be unable to participate fully in worship services since they feel dead inside. At this point many assume that God is punishing them, or that they have committed the unpardonable sin. A Christian will then suffer even greater depressive pain, since not only do they feel cut off from people, but also from God, their last resort for help.

When well-meaning Christian friends find out how depressed the person is, they will suggest a greater commitment to prayer and Bible study as a treatment for the condition. This of course, is impossible, since both acts require a great deal of concentration with which depression always interferes. Unfortunately, this inability to pray and study will indicate to the friends that the depressed person must have a spiritual problem, a lack of faith, or that they don't really want to get well. Self-help books and tapes will then be tried along with perhaps pastoral counselling. These methods only work when a person has total thought control which allows them to change their thinking patterns. When Christian self-help methods fail, the depressed believer will feel so spiritually dead and hopeless that they may give up Christianity completely.

A depressed Christian has additional guilt added to their depression, since they usually condemn themselves for not snapping out of it. They will assume that they have a spiritual weakness or a character flaw. Pastors may have taught them that a true Christian will never get depressed and that it is a sign of defeat, disobedience and unbelief, so they feel increasingly guilty. It will be harder to attend church, since socialization is very difficult, and they feel like hypocrites for not being able to pray, worship or read the Bible. Since concentration is so impaired, they get little out of sermons, so they tend to change churches frequently since they "are not being fed" or the church "isn't meeting their needs." Depression is particularly painful for Christians and there is much unnecessary suffering due to their wrong understanding of mental conditions.

Depression may be slightly more common in Evangelical churches than in the general population since these churches deliberately attract seekers who are looking for answers to life. Depressed people are always seeking for relief, so many will come into our churches. If the seekers are not helped with their depression as well

Depressed Christians often feel beaten up by the church.

as with eternal life, there is a very high rate of "backsliding," since they perceive that Christianity has not meet their needs, and they feel no better.

How does depression affect pastors?

An untreated depressed pastor can cause serious damage to a church and to his own ministry. He will likely label his symptoms as "burnout" and may blame it on the congregation, his spouse or superiors. Most often he will blame himself for sliding into a spiritual valley where prayer and Bible study become very difficult. When the condition doesn't improve using the usual scriptural methods for drawing closer to God, he then will presume that he is too far from God to be helped, and that his "call" or "anointing" has lifted. Pastors are very reluctant to seek help from fellow ministers due to embarrassment, so they suffer in isolation.

If there is mood instability, they may act impulsively and slip into sin. This will then put them under discipline. They will likely then leave the ministry in personal disgrace. This sequence of events can be easily prevented if depression is recognized and treated early.

Traditionally, churches criticize and then expel any leader who seems to be slipping in their attitude or performance. I would like to encourage all Christians to be watching for any signs of depression in their leaders. Instead of criticizing them, offer to support and help them get treated. If treatment can be started early, a pastor may not even need to be away from his pulpit before he returns to full function.

Chapter 12
Why are Christians so difficult to treat?

Mental health problems are poorly understood by the public at large, as we have already discussed. The Christian population is not only equally uninformed, but we have created our own explanation for the causes and treatments of mental illnesses. It is assumed that since spiritual symptoms are present, then there must be a spiritual cause, and that a spiritual treatment will always work. If it doesn't, then the victim is blamed for inadequate faith or motivation. Christians don't realize that depression is the only medical condition with spiritual symptoms.

I WANT TO DIE
I CAN'T GO ON
I CAN'T PRAY
I MUST HAVE SINNED
GOD IS PUNISHING ME
I'M ANGRY
I'M SAD

**Depression is the only medical condition
with spiritual symptoms.**

Christians assume that they are in full control of their thoughts, but this is not so when a mood disorder is present. One's ability to control thoughts depends on how well the brain cells are functioning to give you that control. It is much like the control of a car. One only has full control if the steering wheel is properly connected under the hood. In mood disorders, the problem is not with the will of the person, but with the nerve cells "under the hood."

Christians are very reluctant to seek medical help with their moods, since they perceive that this is an admission that they "don't have enough resources in God," or that "the Cross isn't enough." This is sometimes reinforced by well meaning friends or pastors who intensify their guilt. It is also thought that no medical treatment could ever help a spiritual problem, so it would be an insult to God to accept such treatment.

Another argument used by Christians to discourage the use

Christians are kept from treatment by religious arguments.

of medications, is that when you are on them you become so artificially happy that you no longer face the pain of reality and avoid the inner healing that is necessary for complete emotional wholeness. Christians must realize that antidepressants only give people improved thought control; they do not create artificial happiness. A well-treated person is far better able to face the tough issues after treatment since they will no longer be overwhelmed and paralyzed by life stresses.

Christians need to understand that treatment won't undermine their faith, nor override their will. Antidepressants are not "mood altering drugs" nor are they addicting. It is quite permissible for Christians to take them. Medications are a part of the recovery process along with pastoral counselling, praying for healing and personal devotions.

Everywhere I go speaking on this subject, I am overwhelmed by the number of Christians who are using religious arguments to refuse treatment. Many who are taking medications seem paralyzed by guilt, shame and self-condemnation for accepting medical help. I have met many depressed pastors and evangelists who fear the loss of their ministry position if someone should find out that they take antidepressants. Satan loves this state of affairs. As long as he can use religious arguments to get Christians to believe his lie that they should never consider medical treatment, then he can have easy access to the minds of depressed Christians. Those who do take the treatment and recover are no threat to Satan if he can get them overwhelmed by guilt and shame.

It is my hope that with the information in this book, any pastor or friend will be able to understand depression well enough to know when to recommend that a person seek medical help, and then to support the person in the treatment process. Pastors get worn down by the endless counselling required by medically depressed people who rarely show improvement. Using these tools, a pastor can refer and offer support. He can help the victim understand that this is just another treatable illness. This will give the person a better recovery, and will encourage the pastor rather than exhaust him.

The church should become a place of healing and recovery rather than of condemnation, shame and denial. As Christians, we should be able to offer hope to the depressed. We need to give permission for the depressed to admit their struggles and then have someone come along side them to walk them through recovery. As long as the church remains silent about these issues, many will give up on Christianity, live tormented lives, and some will commit suicide needlessly.

Chapter 13
How can depression be treated?

It's an illness, treat it!

It is important to realize that since depression is an illness, it cannot be fought alone by the patient. It can't be wished away. It needs specific medical treatment to correct the imbalance just like insulin is used to treat diabetes. The most important first step is for the patient to accept the diagnosis and consent to treatment. Even mild chemical depressions can be cleared with medications, so there is no need to wait until one is suicidal to begin treatment.

There are many impediments to treatment. Patients and their families are often afraid of mental health professionals, and so won't come for help. They refuse to accept the diagnosis due to the stigma and stereotypes surrounding mental illnesses and psychiatric treatment.

What do the drugs do?

The medical treatment of mood disorders involves the use of drugs that are extremely effective in restoring the normal balance of neurotransmitter chemicals. For depression, there are nearly thirty medications called antidepressants. They restore brain serotonin levels and correct the imbalance. Concentration, mood and thought control will then be restored and the racing thoughts will stop. For bipolar or manic depressives, the mood stabilizing drugs like Lithium,

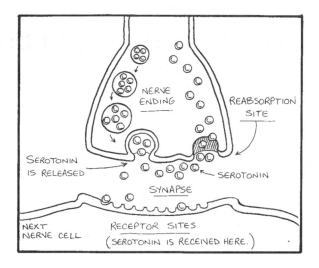

Before treatment, serotonin levels are low.

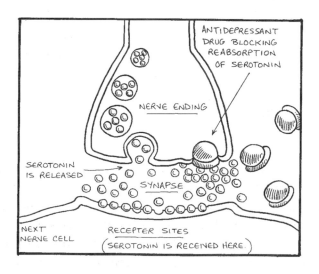

With treatment, serotonin levels are higher.

Valproic Acid, Carbamazapine and others are used to eliminate and prevent mood swings. Some bipolar patients will need to take a combination of stabilizers and antidepressants to prevent both depression and mood swings. If we use the vision analogy again, this is like wearing bifocals – a lens for distance and one for reading.

Most of these medicines have been around for many years and have an excellent track record for long term safety. They are not habit-forming and do not include tranquilizers. They are not "uppers" or "happy pills," they only restore normal mood and the ability to control one's thoughts. They do not create an artificial high, nor artificial personality, and have no effect at all on a person with normal mood.

It is not possible to know in advance which antidepressant medication will work for any given person. Many may have to be tried before finding the right one. The benefit of a pill can take six weeks to feel, which is frustratingly slow. I warn everyone that it may take six to eight months to find the right medication that will give maximum benefit with the least side effects. This process is

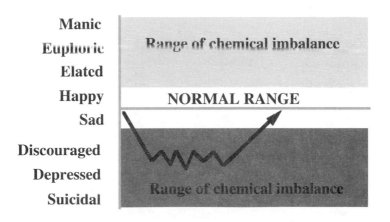

Antidepressants will slowly raise mood by restoring brain chemical balance.

similar to trying to find the right key to open a lock. Many keys may have to be tried before the lock opens. During this waiting period the person needs lots of encouragement to continue trying to find the right medicine.

Once the correct medicine is found, one must stay on it for at least six months after the end of depressive symptoms. This long period lessens the chance of relapse after the medications have been stopped. Statistics have shown that after one episode of depressive illness, fifty percent of recovered people will suffer from another episode within two years. After having two episodes, the risk of relapse within two years increases to seventy percent. After three episodes the relapse risk is ninety percent. It's important that patients recognize the symptoms of relapse early and start treatment as soon as possible. It is generally recommended that the best way to prevent or reduce the risk of relapse is to stay on antidepressant medications indefinitely. For those people who remain on treatment, medications must be considered equivalent to eyeglasses, insulin or heart pills that must be taken for life. These medications are not a

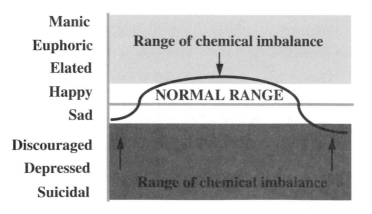

Mood stabilizers will normalize mood swings.

crutch, but they actually correct the problem as long as they are taken continuously.

Unfortunately, the chances that someone will stay on their medications for the correct time period are very low. The drop-out rates from treatment range from ten to seventy percent. This is certainly true in my clinic. The majority of patients will drop out of treatment after three visits to the clinic. The reasons for these bad statistics are many. Often the patient does not accept the reality of the illness and won't take the medications. In other cases friends and family encourage them to stop treatment, or the side effects are intolerable. In any event there are many people who should be in treatment but refuse. It is estimated that only twenty percent of the mood disorder population is receiving treatment.

While I was preparing this book I came across a newspaper article that described the use of antidepressants in animals. It appears that chemical imbalances are found in many mammals. In this article, it explained how veterinarians in the Calgary, Alberta Zoo were using Prozac to help a polar bear stop its "neurotic pacing." The improvement was dramatic, so they are doing a study on the use of antidepressants in animals. We will have to wait and see how pet owners will cope with the stigma of their animals being on mood altering drugs.

You mean I can't drink coffee?

One very important fact that is often overlooked in the treatment of depression is the disruptive role of caffeine and other "over the counter" substances. It has been my observation over the years that caffeine directly opposes the action of antidepressants and mood stabilizers. This is true of all "stimulants" like ginseng, decongestants and many other "natural" products designed to "pick you up," or help you lose weight. In each case the stimulant increases the repetitive, disturbing thoughts that the medications are trying to subdue. Caffeine and other stimulants work directly against the medications. I have been astonished at how much my patients improve when they eliminate caffeine and stimulants from their diets. In some cases I have been able to reduce their doses once the aggravating substance has been removed. I have also noticed that a frustrating tendency for antidepressants to lose their effectiveness over time is reduced if caffeine is eliminated. Caffeine comes in many products, including pain killers, coffee, tea, colas and chocolate. Whenever there is an unexpected decline in the mood of one of my patients, I always look for something they may be consuming that is causing a drug interaction with their medications.

Are tranquilizers ever used?

In many cases tranquilizers are used to temporarily relieve the torment of repetitive, anxious thoughts. They do not correct the underlying imbalance, but cover it over for a short time. These medicines have generic names that commonly end with the letters "..pam," for example "diazepam." Tranquilizers are useful in the short term treatment of an acute episode of anxiety or mood disturbance. They are commonly used for immediate symptom relief while waiting the several weeks it takes for an antidepressant to take effect. Since tranquilizers can be habit-forming, they are usually tapered off as the antidepressant corrects the underlying problem.

Antipsychotic medications are used to stop psychotic symptoms that can occur with severe depression, mania or schizophrenia. They can be combined with antidepressants and stabilizers when necessary.

What is "Shock Treatment"?

Shock treatment is more properly known as E.C.T., electroconvulsive therapy. It was the original treatment for depression but is now rarely used due to the effectiveness of medications.

E.C.T. is the application of an electric shock to one side of the brain to induce a seizure while the person is safely under general anesthesia. The seizure causes a rapid release of all the nerve cell chemicals that are used to regulate brain function. Some of those chemicals are the ones deficient in depression. The sudden release helps correct the chemical imbalance and restores normal mood. Usually up to ten treatments are required to get the chemicals up to the necessary levels to restore mood. Antidepressant medications are often used to maintain the recovery after E.C.T.

E.C.T. is now generally used only in those who do not respond to medications. It is a safe and rapidly effective treatment. I have had suicidal patients recover dramatically within two weeks of having E.C.T. after failing to improve on medications. Please don't ever discourage someone from accepting this form of treatment since it could save their lives.

What about the families?

One very often overlooked part of the treatment of depression is the support that is needed for the families of depressed people. These families are living under severe relationship stress and need to understand the illness and how it is treated. They must be helped with the guilt that they carry for having this problem in their family.

Personal and family counselling is a very important part of the treatment. There are usually many scars to heal as a result of psychological trauma and conflict. Counselling works best after the depressed person has regained control of their thoughts and concentration. Friends and counsellors can be very helpful in supporting the person while they are waiting for the medications to work.

Support groups are now widely available for those suffering with emotional disorders. I have found them to be extremely helpful in providing education to the patient and their families. Perhaps their greatest value however, is to provide encouragement to the sufferer to persist with treatment until they have recovered.

What can you do?

If you are a friend or loved one of someone suffering from a mental illness, you can play a pivotal role in your loved one's recovery. The most important way you can help is by encouraging the person to get help and to stay in treatment even during the frustrating weeks needed to find the right medications. You can be a constant encouragement for them to go on. You can keep reminding them that this is a medical problem, that it's not their fault.

The treatment of depression involves both medications and counselling. All those involved in treatment should work together and support the efforts of the others. Competition between treatment modalities is unhealthy and has caused many to give up treatment altogether.

With correct treatment and supportive family and friends, a depressed person can become relaxed, content, optimistic and in full control of their thoughts and behaviors.

Chapter 14

What is A.D.D. or hyperactivity?

Why is this so controversial?

Attention Deficit Disorder (A.D.D.) has become one of the most controversial and emotionally charged subjects in medicine, education and child rearing. The public, and even the medical profession, are divided into several groups. One group says that A.D.D. really doesn't exist, it's just bad parenting, bad environment, poor social skills and not enough discipline. This group feels that medical treatment is not only unnecessary, but it is a cruel way of suppressing a child and excusing the parent or teacher from their child rearing or teaching responsibilities. Another group feels that A.D.D. is a common physical handicap that needs to be treated medically just like poor vision is treated in children. Yet another group feels that it should only be treated with natural herbs, vitamins and diets.

Just as in every other area of psychiatry, the root cause of the controversy is our inability to measure mood, thought speed, and concentration. We have no reliable, objective test to tell if a person has A.D.D. or any other mental health condition. Whenever something cannot be proven, it will be the subject of speculation. Once again we rely on a checklist of symptoms that when present, indicate a high likelihood that a chemical imbalance is present. There are many in medicine and in the public who cannot accept that a checklist of symptoms is sufficient grounds to initiate drug treatment in a child or adult.

I hope this chapter will introduce you to this subject and clear up much of the confusion surrounding such a common handicap.

What is A.D.D.?

Attention Deficit Disorder (A.D.D.) simply means that a person has a chronic inability to concentrate or focus their mind. It usually presents in one of two ways, with hyperactivity (A.D.H.D.) or without. This is the most common thinking problem in children, and it is estimated that six percent of children suffer from it. It is a leading cause of school failure and underachievement. At least fifty percent of the affected children will never be diagnosed or treated, so they remain disabled, often for life.

The normal brain seems to have filters or gates that allow you to block useless information or stimuli that could distract you from an intended task. In A.D.D. the filters are so weak that the child is bombarded with useless and irrelevant thoughts that are continuously distracting them from learning and remembering. It is very much like being in a small room with many loudspeakers all

"They are constantly being distracted by too many thoughts."

shouting instructions and not being able to tell which voice is the important one. The child finds that their brain tells them too many things at once, and they don't know how to process all the commands. For example, as you read this page, you are likely not aware of the street noises or even the buzz of the lights or fans in your room until I draw your attention to them. Your thoughts are focused on what you are reading. In A.D.D. a person's thoughts are going so fast that they are not able to concentrate on the page, and the environmental noises are just as important as what they are reading. The brain can not prioritize what the most important stimulus is at any moment. The street noise becomes as important as the page, and the mind is distracted to the noise so the reading is never completed. That is why distractibility is such an important symptom in A.D.D.

A.D.D. is a severe handicap to learning, and is often found in addition to learning disabilities. When new information is learned by a person with normal concentration, it is stored in the memory at a location where it can be easily retrieved for future use. You might say the information is filed in a drawer labeled with the appropriate subject, so when it is needed, the memory can be easily retrieved, since it is well marked. In A.D.D. there is no such filing system. New information just seems to be tossed over the shoulder into a pile of memories. It is virtually impossible to retrieve the information even though you know it's in there somewhere.

This inability to concentrate is caused by an inherited chemical imbalance in the brain, just like the one which causes adult mood disorders. Children have the same racing of thoughts but they are less likely to have the mood symptoms. Their thought clutter is of a more random nature, where the adult pattern has more anxious and depressing thoughts. It is very common to find both A.D.D. and mood disorders clustering in families, since they are closely related conditions that are both inherited.

There are many symptoms of A.D.D. and not every affected child will have all of them. Children may have any of the following symptoms: not finishing what they start, fidgety, distractible, hearing but not listening, unable to concentrate on school work, making noises in class, falling grades, acting like they are driven by a motor, unable to sit still, loud, always talking and impulsive. They are excitable, unable to share, impatient and demanding of their own way with wide mood swings. In a classroom they appear to be daydreaming or disruptive, unable to apply themselves to a task and easily confused by details. They rarely follow instructions, and have exceedingly short memories. There is usually considerable moodiness with extreme emotional responses to events. The irritability, impulsivity and immaturity make it hard for them to make or keep friends, so they become socially isolated. This causes great frustration that leads to impulsive and socially inappropriate behavior.

They usually have poor grades, since school is such a struggle. They need constant supervision and assistance to complete a task or learn a skill. They are often in trouble with authorities and are automatically blamed for anything that goes wrong. These pressures cause the child to lose all self esteem and feel rejected. They become sullen and withdrawn as they get older. In this way A.D.D. is often seen with depression, anxiety and learning disabilities. Twenty five percent of learning disabled children also have A.D.D.

These children are usually of normal intelligence, but they are unable to perform and make use of their abilities. This condition is much like having a high performance sports car ready to go inside a garage but having no driveway to get it on the road. There's great potential but no performance.

How can A.D.D. be treated?

Fifty to eighty percent of A.D.D. children are never diagnosed or treated. For those who are identified, the treatment involves a multifaceted approach. I have not found dietary restrictions to be consistently helpful, but medications are extremely useful. As in adult mood disorders, the drugs will correct the chemical imbalance and restore normal thought speed and sequence. There are many medications that are helpful including stimulants and antidepressants. Many drugs may need to be tried before the right combination is found, though eighty percent of children will respond to stimulants like Methylphenidate (Ritalin). The medications will reduce impulsivity and hyperactivity by slowing down the speed of their thoughts. At a more normal thought speed, it is easier to control thoughts and behavior. Concentration, learning, self confidence and mood will improve as thought control increases. Treatment can release a child from the prison of thought bombardment so that he is able to choose his own thoughts at his own speed and focus his attention at will.

Parents are generally very reluctant to accept the diagnosis or give pills to their children for this condition. This is very understandable, since no one wants to see their child on medications. The fact is however, that with medications the child will be happier and calmer with better performance and self esteem. This will greatly improve home life and family relationships. I encourage parents to consider Methylphenidate (Ritalin) to be equivalent to eyeglasses or insulin which no parent would deny their child. It must be understood that A.D.D. is a medical problem with behavioral symptoms that will respond to treatment.

Physicians who treat A.D.D. with medications are widely criticized for medicating children "needlessly." Having seen the family disruption, educational failures and the personality injury to those children who have not been treated, it is my opinion that it is more dangerous and unfair to deny treatment to an A.D.D. child than to give them medications. When I am in doubt of the diagnosis, I choose to err on the side of offering hope and treatment, than to tell a parent there is nothing that can be done for their child. The risks of medications are very low, but the consequences of missing the diagnosis and leaving a child untreated to face the long term disability of A.D.D.

are enormous.

The education professionals can be very helpful in tailoring a program for the affected child. Limiting distractions in a classroom and seating the child at the front of the class can be very helpful. Giving instructions frequently and in clear simple terms will help these children respond better. Firm and consistent discipline is necessary, though rarely effective, if used alone. A.D.D. children need lots of praise and encouragement for the tasks that they do well. Self esteem must be preserved.

Parents are usually exasperated and very embarrassed by their children's behavior over which they seem to have no control. We must reach out to these parents and try to assist them, rather than join the many friends and neighbours who condemn them for poor parenting. Individual and family counselling is very helpful for these troubled families and individuals. Support groups like "Children and Adults with Attention Deficit Disorder" (CH.A.D.D.) can be a lifeline of help for parents struggling to cope and understand. There are many helpful parenting strategies that can be learned in support groups. Medications are but one of many helpful interventions in A.D.D.

Chapter 15
What happens if you don't treat A.D.D?

Mr. B. was 21 years old when he first came to my office. Throughout junior grade school he had been fidgety, disorganized, concentrating poorly, and with low grades, so he was diagnosed with a learning disability. He was in university when I met him. He was sent to see me by the school counsellor who suspected A.D.D.

As an adult, he continued to have the same difficulty and symptoms that he had as a child. What was new however, were his mood swings. Since his teens he described recurring episodes when his mood would be very elevated with high energy, ambition, optimism, impulsivity and racing thoughts of great plans and ideas. These episodes would be followed by a plunge into despair, low energy, low ambition and racing negative depressing thoughts.

Mr. B. was demonstrating a very typical life history of A.D.D. symptoms as a child that continued into adulthood. After adolescence he developed symptoms of what was clearly bipolar mood disorder along with the A.D.D.

He was treated with mood stabilizers and his grades went from failing, to a "B" average within a few months. His moods stabilized, and he became a consistently pleasant, happy person, delighted with his new academic success. He still had a learning disability, but it was much easier to deal with. With the use of mood stabilizers, both his symptoms of A.D.D. and mood disorder improved. Concentration can be improved with the use of antidepressants or mood stabilizers, with or without stimulants. In adults, I treat the mood first, then add stimulants if necessary for concentration.

It used to be thought that A.D.D. ended in adolescence. It is now known that in forty to sixty percent of cases, the condition continues on into adulthood.

When children with A.D.D. go untreated, they may become sullen, with low self-esteem, withdrawn, irritable, rebellious and conditioned for failure. They then associate with other kids with the same disability, since they are rejected by their peers who can't tolerate their impulsive behavior. In their teens they may become rebellious, defiant and often have trouble with the law. When experimenting with drugs and alcohol, they notice for the first time that they are able to relax and concentrate until the drink wears off. They then continue to drink because it is the first time in their lives that they have been able to have control of their thoughts. There is a very high incidence of drug and alcohol addiction among untreated A.D.D. and mood-disordered adults. Chronic use of these substances will actually make the chemical imbalance worse.

With age, the hyperactive symptoms decline, but the mood symptoms increase, so there is a very high incidence of depression, anxiety and mood swings added to the inability to concentrate. Untreated A.D.D. may lead to a lifetime of blame, shame, failure, anger, social isolation, restlessness, underemployment, relationship failure, drug and alcohol abuse and mood disorder. They lead disorganized lives, forgetful, chronically late, poor time managers, frequently change jobs, homes and spouses. They have severe interpersonal problems due to impulsiveness and intolerance of the opinions of others. This condition affects every aspect of life and personality. I consider it urgent to treat anyone suspected of A.D.D. as soon as the diagnosis is made.

Adults with A.D.D. are often discovered when they bring their own children in for an A.D.D. assessment. At that time the parent may recognize that they too have had the same symptoms their whole life.

Adults can be treated with Methylphenidate (Ritalin) but more often with antidepressants and mood stabilizers. Counselling is very important for the adult with A.D.D. since there is usually so much emotional hurt and scarring to overcome before progress can be made.

Treatment will make these people more relaxed, tolerant, dependable, confident, happy, with good self control and self esteem

A.D.D. is a very large subject that can never be adequately covered in a small book like this one. There are many very helpful books that have been written on the subject and the internet is full of information. I encourage you to read further into this subject if you recognize yourself or a loved one in the symptom list.

Chapter 16
What is schizophrenia?

Mrs. L. was a patient in hospital that I was asked to see because she was thinking strangely. She was very quiet, withdrawn and suspicious of me. When I asked her what was the reason that she was in hospital, she replied, "I'm rotting inside because I was standing too close to wallpaper that was peeling off the wall." She had clearly lost contact with reality but I needed to know how firmly convinced of her delusion she was. I asked her if this had ever happened before. She answered, "Yes it had but she had acted quickly and saved her own life." "And how did you do that?" I responded. She showed me a twelve inch scar across her neck. "When the poison was beginning to move towards my head, I cut my neck to let the poison out and saved my life!" She was clearly quite convinced of her diagnosis and of the treatment she needed. I cringed as I thought of the doctors who had to close such an enormous life threatening neck wound, while she was so proud of her life saving procedure. Mrs. L. was schizophrenic and demonstrating psychotic delusional thinking.

Schizophrenia is a very misunderstood condition, and it is not "split personality." It is a "psychotic" disorder, rather than a mood disorder, which means that there is a loss of contact with reality. It is caused by a different type of chemical imbalance than a mood disorder. Schizophrenia is a thought disorder where one loses the ability to tell what is real and what is imaginary. If you refer back to my diagram on page 19, this disorder is a chemical imbalance in the

the orientation part of the brain, but it can also affect the mood control centre to cause mood symptoms as well.

Schizophrenia usually begins in young adults like other mood disorders. It affects two percent of the population, which makes it more common and far more disabling than diabetes. Like the mood disorders, it tends to be a recurring condition.

Schizophrenics often feel that they are being watched, followed or persecuted. They may hear voices and see things that no one else can. They often have peculiar beliefs that have no basis in reality and their thoughts seem very scattered and disorganized. They are commonly very withdrawn, emotionless and suspicious. A more complete list of symptoms will be found in chapter 20.

Schizophrenia is a more difficult condition to treat than the mood disorders, and the medications, called antipsychotics, tend to have more side effects. Antidepressants and mood stabilizers can also be used in schizophrenia if there are many depressive thoughts

Delusional psychotic thinking.

or wide mood swings along with the psychosis. Antipsychotics are also used in mood disorders when the person is having symptoms of psychosis along with their mood symptoms.

We must be very compassionate and supportive to schizophrenics and their families to keep the sufferer encouraged and in treatment to prevent relapses.

There are very helpful support groups for patients and families to encourage and inform those who suffer with this condition.

Chapter 17

What is anxiety disorder and obsessive compulsive disorder (O.C.D.)?

Anxiety disorders are conditions that interfere with your ability to control or stop a sense of continuous worry or fear. They are very common, and have the same incidence and lifetime risk as the mood disorders. Anxiety disorders are commonly found with depression, since the continuous anxious thoughts are just another form of negative thoughts that can't be shut off. In my opinion, anxiety appears to be a subtype of the depressive mood disorder, since they both have negative thoughts that can't be controlled, and they both respond to the same medications.

There are several types of anxiety disorders. Panic disorder is the most severe and disabling of these conditions. In this disorder, panic attacks will start with no obvious trigger. There will be sudden unexplained terror and a sense of impending doom. There will be many physical symptoms that occur simultaneously like a pounding heart, sweating, chest pain and light headedness. Phobic disorder is when a person will become very fearful or even panic over a well defined object or situation like heights, snakes or crowds. General anxiety disorder is when a person is worried all the time about everything.

"Anxious thoughts often can't be stopped."

Obsessive Compulsive Disorder (O.C.D.)

Obsessive Compulsive Disorder (O.C.D.) is quite a common disabling disorder. Three percent of the population will suffer from it at some time in their lives. It is more common than schizophrenia or manic depression, but it is well concealed and rarely diagnosed.

Obsessional thoughts are recurrent, intrusive, unwanted ideas, images, impulses or worries that are often senseless, but can't be shut off. They will often take the form of swear words, repetitive phrases, violent thoughts that are totally out of character, or feelings of being dirty or contaminated. This is very disturbing for the victim who feels powerless to control the thoughts. The anxiety associated with O.C.D. can be overwhelming.

Compulsions are repetitive unnecessary acts done in response to the obsessional thoughts. They are intended to neutralize the fear or discomfort that comes with the obsessional thoughts. These acts are purposeless, time consuming and unwanted. They are very disruptive to relationships and to one's performance at home or work. The acts usually involve excessive touching, checking, cleaning, washing, counting or note taking. The victim hates doing it, but must continue the act until they get a sense of completion which may require a large number of repetitions. During the compulsion there is never a sense that the action has been completed correctly. Some have described it like an itch that won't go away until it is scratched a certain way and a certain number of times.

The most common obsessions are fear of contamination by dirt or germs, fear of harm to self or others, fear of illness, fear of sexual thoughts, and fear of committing sins. The most common repetitive rituals to suppress the fearful thoughts are repetitive cleaning, recitation of a phrase or number, touching, checking of locks, excessive orderliness and hoarding. It is not uncommon for someone with O.C.D. to wash their hands thirty times a day to stop the fear of contamination.

Anxiety and depression are often so intertwined that they are indistinguishable. In my clinic I have not found it necessary to separate the conditions. They both have negative thoughts that can't be shut off, and they both respond to the same antidepressants which are designed to restore thought control.

Chapter 18
What can be done for anorexia nervosa, chronic fatigue and fibromyalgia?

A person suffering from anorexia is obsessed with unwanted continuous negative thoughts of being too fat. They will be unable to stop worrying about their weight, so dieting becomes a compulsion that can't be controlled. Dieting to the point of starvation often takes place, since the thoughts won't quit, and the victim can never be satisfied that an acceptable weight has been reached.

Thirty to fifty percent of those with anorexia also suffer from mood disorders, since both conditions are caused by a chemical imbalance that allows the mind to fill with negative thoughts. Antidepressants can correct the imbalance and restore normal mood and thought control. This will allow the person to accept and restore a normal weight and eating pattern. Counselling is also necessary and helpful with all of these disorders.

The list of symptoms which define Chronic Fatigue Syndrome are very similar to those of depression. Antidepressants can help with the depressive symptoms of the syndrome so that considerable relief can be obtained.

Fibromyalgia is a condition which, among other things, involves chronic muscle pain, sleep disturbance and depression. It is known that sixty percent of those with chronic pain will also have a chemical imbalance depression. The depression can be a result of the chronic pain, or the pain can be a result of chronic depression.

Fibromyalgia will often improve with the use of antidepressants which can improve sleep, relax muscles and give some pain relief. The benefits can be seen even without depressive symptoms being present.

It is easy to scc that antidepressants have very wide uses in any condition where unwanted thoughts disrupt concentration or behavior.

Chapter 19
Conclusion

It is important for the public to realize that a person with depression, mania, anxiety and attention deficit is helplessly in the grip of an illness that he can't control. These conditions are legitimate physical problems with medical treatments just like diabetes or any other chronic illness. It is unfair the way these people are treated with fear, suspicion, hushed embarrassment and condemnation. Most of these people can be totally controlled with medication and returned to a normal productive life. Christians must realize that these are very common treatable physical illnesses which can affect anyone through no fault of their own.

Our communities and churches are full of hurting people looking for answers to life's struggles. Many of them will have mood disorders needing treatment. They are hurt when friends or pastors declare that depression is a sign of weakness or deficient faith. A depressed person should never be told to "snap out of it" any more than a diabetic should be told to "smarten up and stop using Insulin."

Many are suffering needlessly from depression and other mood disorders. They are unaware that safe, effective treatment is available. and acceptable for Christians. Through public education, more depressed people will realize their need for treatment, and they will no longer see themselves as social outcasts. People with mood disorders need to be encouraged to recognize the problem and get help.

This book can help a person diagnose the kind of disorder

they have, and discover what treatments are available. The symptom checklist in chapter 20 is a summary of the symptoms of chemical imbalance of mood control. If you are wondering if you or a family member are suffering from a mood disorder, then just compare yourself with the symptoms in the checklist. If you have a number of the symptoms, then take the list to a physician and discuss how you are feeling, so that a treatment plan can be started.

God has called us to lead our world out of the bondage of sin, let us also minister release to those of our members bound in the captivity of their minds.

Chapter 20
Symptom Checklist

Compare yourself to the symptoms listed below. If you see yourself being described, you should take this list to your physician and discuss it with him.

Depression or Anxiety:

At least five of the following symptoms need to be present every day for at least two weeks with no other personal situation present (like grief), or a medical condition like drugs or low thyroid, that may be causing the symptoms:

1. Persistent sad, anxious, or "empty" mood, most of the time, most days.
2. Feelings of hopelessness, pessimism and low self esteem.
3. Feelings of guilt, worthlessness, helplessness.
4. Loss of interest or pleasure in hobbies and activities that were once enjoyed,including sex.
5. Insomnia, early-morning awakening or oversleeping.
6. Loss of appetite and/or weight loss or overeating and weight gain.
7. Decreased energy, fatigue, feeling "slowed down" or agitation that can't be controlled.
8. Procrastination, since simple tasks seem harder.
9. Thoughts of death or suicide, suicide attempts, constant

feelings of "life isn't worth living like this."

10. Restlessness, irritability, bad temper, inability to relax or be content.
11. Difficulty concentrating, remembering and making decisions due to persistent uncontrollable cluttering of down, sad, negative thoughts that can't be kept out of the mind.

Other common symptoms of depression are:

12. Persistent physical symptoms that do not respond to treatment, such as headaches, digestive disorders, and chronic pain.
13. Continuous anxiety that can't be turned off. Uncontrollable worry about small things, including physical health.
14. Social isolation or withdrawal due to increasing difficulty to make small talk.
15. Other relatives with depression, alcoholism or nervous breakdowns.
16. In children, look for increased irritability, persisting complaints of physical problems, agitation and unwarranted anxiety or panic, or social withdrawal.

Adolescent Depression:

1. Depressed mood or irritability that may lead to antisocial or rebellious behavior.
2. Unstable mood that changes rapidly even with insignificant events.
3. Poor concentration, drop in school performance, skipping school.
4. Loss of interest in school or friends, social withdrawal even

   from family.
5.   Inability to stop worrying.
6.   Inability to sleep, or always oversleeping to escape.
7.   Over or undereating.
8.   Too much restless energy, or always overtired.
9.   Inability to enjoy things that they used to find pleasurable.
10.   Many physical complaints like muscle pains, headaches, abdominal pains.
11.   Feeling picked on or that everyone is against them.
12.   Inappropriate guilt, shame and blame.
13.   Increased use of street drugs or alcohol to self medicate.
14.   Loss of interest in own appearance and personal hygiene.

Dysthymia:

Dysthymia is a milder form of depression that is just as treatable as Depression and with the same medications.

1.   Depressed mood most of the time for most days for at least two years with at least two of the following:
2.   Poor appetite or overeating.
3.   Insomnia or oversleeping.
4.   Low energy, always tired.
5.   Low self esteem.
6.   Poor concentration and difficulty making decisions.
7.   Feeling hopeless.
8.   These symptoms interfere with social or vocational function.

Obsessive Compulsive Disorder:

1.   Recurring persistent and intrusive disturbing thoughts that cause anxiety and distress.

2. The thoughts are unrelated to actual events.
3. The person tries to stop the thoughts with another thought or action.
4. The person is aware that the thoughts are untrue and from his own mind.
5. Repetitive, meaningless behaviors (hand washing, ordering, checking) or thought rituals (praying, counting, repetitions) that they must do to neutralize the unwanted disturbing thoughts.
6. The thoughts and resulting actions are time consuming, disruptive and embarrassing to the person but they have no control over them.

Mania or Hypomania (mild mania), indicating Bipolar Disorder

1. Exaggerated elation, rapid unpredictable mood changes.
2. Irritability, impatience with others who can't keep up with them.
3. Inability to sleep, not needing sleep, too busy to sleep and not being tired the next day.
4. Big plans, inflated self esteem, exaggerated self importance, impulsive overspending.
5. Increased talking, louder and faster, and can't stop.
6. Racing and jumbled thoughts, topics changing rapidly; no one can keep up.
7. Poor concentration, distractibility.
8. Increased sexual desire, uninhibited, acting out of character or promiscuous.
9. Markedly increased energy, "can't be stopped," erratic aggressive driving.
10. Poor judgment, no insight, refusing treatment, blaming others.

11. Inappropriate high risk social behavior, brash, telling people off, overreaction to events, misinterpreting events, distortion of meaning of ordinary remarks.
12. Lasts hours to days, usually ending with a crash into profound depression.
13. Not caused by street drugs like "Speed" or Cocaine.

Attention Deficit Disorder

Without hyperactivity

A.D.D. may be mild, moderate or severe, so these symptoms may only be present mildly. As in the other mood disorders, everyone is affected differently.

One may display six or more of these symptoms daily for more than six months:
1. Racing cluttered thoughts causing constant thought distractions, making victims very susceptible to any distraction.
2. No attention to details; lots of careless errors.
3.. Inability to complete tasks, since they can't pay attention long enough to remember or follow instructions.
4. Hearing, but not listening, even when spoken to directly.
5. Unable to concentrate on school work unless with one-on-one attention.
6. Making purposeless noises to fill any silence.
7. Falling grades, disruptive in class, defiant of authority, disorganized.
8. Daydreaming, losing things, forgetful.
9. Sometimes shy and withdrawn.

With Hyperactivity

1. Fidgets and squirms.
2. Can't remain seated in classroom.
3. Excessive running and climbing when inappropriate.
4. Can't do anything quietly.
5. Always in motion as if "driven by a motor."
6. Can't stop talking.
7. Blurts out answers before question is completed.
8. Unable to wait a turn and easily frustrated.
9. Often interrupting and intruding, impulsive and disruptive.
10. Difficulty making or keeping friends, unable to share, demanding their own way, impatient, poor losers and generally socially immature.
11. Exaggerated emotional response to both good and bad events with wide mood swings.

There will often be a family history of A.D.D., depression, other mood disorders, or alcoholism in relatives of an A.D.D. child.

Adult A.D.D.

1. Chronic forgetfulness.
2. Problems with time and money management.
3. Disorganized lifestyle.
4. Frequent moves or job changes.
5. Periodic depression, mood swings or anxiety as in the mood disorders above.
6. Chronic patterns of under-achievement.
7. Feelings of restlessness.
8. Impulsive behavior.
9. Tendency toward substance abuse.
10. Low self esteem.

11.   May be over/under reactive.

12.   Easily frustrated.

13.   Difficulty concentrating

14.   Difficulty maintaining relationships

15.   Often labeled as lazy, immature, daydreamer, quitter or having a bad attitude.

Schizophrenia or any psychotic breakdown

1.   Emotionally flat and withdrawn, or very excited, hostile or grandiose.

2.   Poor verbal communication, disorganized, unconnected thoughts.

3.   Delusional thinking; believing something to be true that is outside the realm of reason, and for which there is no real evidence – often religious.

4.   Seeing things not visible to others, or hearing things not audible to others.

5.   Feelings of being watched or followed by other individuals or organizations.

6.   There are many complex symptoms in psychotic illnesses needing professional   assessment. Basically, during a psychotic episode a person loses touch with reality and is unable to function in their normal life activities. If you see this symptom, the person needs urgent medical attention.

The information contained in this booklet is for educational purposes only and does not replace the medical evaluation of a physician.

These checklists are adapted from:
The American Psychiatric Association: Diagnostic and Statistical Manual of Mental Disorders, Fourth Edition.
Washington, D.C. American Psychiatric Association, 1994

About Dr. Grant Mullen

Dr. Grant Mullen is a mental health physician in Ontario, Canada. He has a special interest in depression, mood swings, anxiety disorders and how these conditions affect Christians.

Dr. Mullen lectures internationally on how medical treatment can be successfully combined with emotional and spiritual healing to break the chains of emotional and mental bondage. He has written a number of books, and has produced many audio and video tapes. You can learn more about Dr. Mullen, order materials, and read his e-magazine on, emotional recovery, at www.drgrantmullen.com.

For a more complete discussion of emotional recovery in body, soul and spirit, see Dr. Mullen's book, *Emotionally Free*. (Published in North America by Chosen Books and internationally by Sovereign World, ISBN 1 85240 365 9.)